# Ayurvedic Nutrition

## A Guide to Conscious Eating

By Dr. Nibodhi Haas

Mata Amritanandamayi Center
San Ramon, California, United States

# Ayurvedic Nutrition

by Nibodhi and Gunavati
Published by:
>Mata Amritanandamayi Center
>P.O. Box 613
>San Ramon, CA 94583
>United States

Copyright © 2014 2014 by by Mata Amritanandamayi Center, San Ramon, California, USA

All rights reserved. No part of this publication may be stored in a retrieval system, transmitted, reproduced, transcribed or translated into any language, in any form, by any means without the prior agreement and written permission of the publisher.

In India:
>www.amritapuri.org
>inform@amritapuri.org

In USA:
>www.amma.org

In Europe:
>www.amma-europe.org

The information in this book is not intended to diagnose, treat, cure, or prevent any disease or disorder. It is intended for educational purposes only.

*It is our sincere prayer that this book is of service to the reader, humanity, and Mother Nature. May it bring health and happiness. Any benefit derived from this information is due to Amma's infinite grace and compassion, as well as the wisdom of the ancient Rishis (Seers). Any mistakes within this text are the responsibility of the authors. This book is offered at the lotus feet of our beloved Satguru, Sri Mata Amritanandamayi.*

# Table of Contents

| | |
|---|---:|
| Introduction | 5 |
| Balancing Your Diet | 8 |
| Determining Prakriti: Your Individual Constitution | 10 |
| Vata-Pacifying Diet | 12 |
| Pitta-Pacifying Diet | 15 |
| Kapha-Pacifying Diet | 17 |
| Food Combining Chart | 19 |
| Acidity & Alkalinity | 21 |
| Organic Food | 23 |
| Water: The Fountain of Life | 27 |
| Activating & Revitalizing Food | 28 |
| Common Food Allergies | 29 |
| What's That on Your Plate? | 40 |
| Dharmic Dining | 50 |
| Ending World Hunger | 56 |
| Eating Up Resources | 58 |
| Vitamins & Nutrients | 60 |
| Body Care & Household Cleaning Products | 64 |
| Fasting for Health | 68 |
| Panchakarma Dietary Suggestions | 70 |
| Eating with Awareness | 73 |
| Foods for Healing Illness | 77 |
| Conclusion | 82 |
| Suggested Reading | 84 |

# Introduction

*"The ayurvedic physician begins the cure of disease by arranging the diet that is to be followed by the patient. Ayurvedic physicians rely so much on diet that it is declared that all diseases can be cured by following dietetic rules carefully along with the proper herbal supplements; but if a patient does not attend to his diet, a hundred good medicines will not cure him."*

– Charaka Samhita 1.41

Health and happiness are nourished and sustained by proper food and attitude. Ancient cultures and schools of healing understand that physical and emotional health are significantly affected by the foods we choose to consume. Natural foods, prepared with love and awareness, cultivate health in the body and mind. Foods filled with toxic thoughts or substances – such as bleaching agents, artificial colors, preservatives, and additives – strain the organs. When the bodily systems are under stress from unhealthy foods, there is also an emotional result. Chinese medicine makes a correlation between anger and liver toxicity, while grief is associated with lung weakness. Naturopathy shows us how food allergies often result in lethargy, dullness, and even depression.

## Ayurvedic Nutrition

The science of ayurveda teaches that right diet is the foundation of health. Ayurveda classifies the body into three constitutional types or doshas: vata, pitta, and kapha. The term vata refers to the wind and ether elements. Pitta refers to fire and water. Kapha refers to water and earth. Based on their attributes, foods are also classified into three categories: rajasic (agitated/active), tamasic (heavy/dull), and sattvic (light/pure). If we eat rajasic, tamasic, or sattvic food, we can see a similar effect in the body and mind. Through various paths, the same conclusion has been evident: we literally are what we eat.

Ayurvedic dietary guidelines are designed to restore the balance of the doshas. This is essential for maintaining physical vitality, emotional health, and peace of mind. Ayurvedic diets are personalized, based on each individual's constitution. Each individual has unique combinations of the elements and doshas; therefore, ayurvedic dietary requirements also vary. When choosing which foods will be harmonizing, one must consider the individual's constitution, the season, weather, time of the day, quality of the food, as well as one's mental and emotional attitudes at the time of hunger. When ingesting food, we participate in the creative process of nature. With the foods we choose, we can rejuvenate or weaken the entire body.

## Introduction

How we eat is equally as important as what we are eating. If we feel emotionally unbalanced when we eat, the food may disrupt the body's harmony. If we eat too quickly or overeat, the poorly digested end product predisposes us to ill health. Eating in a calm manner with a sense of gratitude will contribute to well-being and coherence in the body.

Following an ayurvedic diet is not difficult. For every food that aggravates particular doshas, there are plenty of alternative, beneficial, and tasty foods that can bring balance. As we attune to what is truly going on in our bodies, we often begin to crave more natural, simple foods. Detrimental eating habits are usually a result of past conditioning by family, friends, and society, and can be replaced by making more self-nurturing choices. Sometimes, making even a few simple changes in diet will bring about a dramatic shift in health.

The entire web of life is affected by our food choices. Choosing wholesome food is one of the best tools we have to create strong bodies and balanced minds, while honoring our Mother Earth and respecting all of her creatures. We encourage you to become aware of the impact your dietary decisions create within your own being and upon the earth. May this information bring understanding and inspiration to fuel ourselves with healthy foods, thereby enabling these bodies to be better vehicles for service and consciousness.

# Balancing Your Diet

Because ayurveda understands the body in terms of a constitutional model, recommendations will usually differ for each person. Ayurveda explains that there are elemental forces that influence nature and human beings. The universe is made up of five great elements: space, wind, fire, water, and earth. All of creation is a dance or play of these five elements. They interact together to make up the three doshas (the bodily humors – vata, pitta and kapha). The word dosha actually means "impurity" or "imbalance." The doshas are responsible for biological, psychological, and physiological processes in our body, mind and consciousness. When in harmony, the doshas sustain balance within us. We all have each of the doshas within us in different proportions/relationships.

Benefits of a eating according to your dosha (constitution) are:

*Balancing Your Diet*

- Better health, youthfulness, and better memory
- More energy, endurance, and strength
- A decrease in existing imbalances
- Prevention of imbalances
- Greater ability to handle stress and anxiety
- Improved sleep and concentration
- Better digestion, metabolism, and elimination
- Healthier skin and complexion
- Slowing down of the aging process
- Healthier children
- Stronger immune system

- Weight balance
- Better meditation and yoga practice

The following survey can give you an idea of your predominant dosha(s). Please keep in mind, this is a very general overview. The best way to determine your dosha/ideal diet, is to visit a qualified ayurvedic practitioner.

# Determining Prakriti: Your Individual Constitution

| Aspects | Vata | Pitta | Kapha |
|---|---|---|---|
| Mental | quick, restless | sharp, aggressive | calm, steady, stable |
| Memory | short term | good | long term |
| Emotions | fear, insecure | anger, irritable | attached, greed |
| Thoughts | changing | usually steady | steady |
| Concentration | short term | above average | long term |
| Dreams | fear, active | anger, fiery | watery, calm |
| Sleep | light, disturbed | sound, medium | deep, long |
| Talking | rapid, scattered | clear, fast, sharp | slow, clear, sweet |
| Voice | high pitch, feeble | medium | low pitch |

## Determining Prakriti: Your Individual Constitution

| Body Frame | thin | medium | large |
|---|---|---|---|
| Body Weight | low | moderate | heavy |
| Skin | dry, rough | soft, oily | thick, oily |
| Hair Type | dry | medium | oily |
| Hair Color | red/grey | dark/light | brown, black |
| Hair Quantity | average | thin | thick |
| Teeth | protruding, crooked | medium, soft | large, strong |
| Eyes | small, dry, active | sharp, penetrating | big, attractive |
| Appetite | low, variable | strong | steady |
| Disease Pattern | nervous, pain | heat related | mucous |
| Thirst | variable | excessive | slight |
| Elimination | dry, hard, constipation | oily, loose, soft | oily, thick, slow |
| Activity | very active | moderate | slow |
| Endurance | fair | good | high |
| Strength | fair | above average | excellent |
| Pulse | snake, feeble | frog, moderate | swan, broad |
|  | thready | jumping | slow |
| **Totals:** | **Vata:** | **Pitta:** | **Kapha:** |

Dosha-specific diets are intended to bring the doshas into harmony in the body, based on one's constitution and current imbalances. For example, if you have predominantly vata characteristics, or if you have vata-related symptoms/disease, it is best to follow the vata-pacifying diet. Please remember these are general, overall guidelines. Dietary requirements will vary according to season, age, digestive capacity, location, and climate. It is often necessary to combine principles from all the doshas based on current individual needs. These guidelines are a good starting point. These lists intentionally do not include meat products and eggs, as they will be discussed in later chapters.

# Vata Pacifying Diet

Vata season is the cold, windy, and dry season. This is when the qualities of vata increase naturally, and one should take extra care to maintain balance during this time. In this period, it is beneficial to take lots of warm food and drinks, heavier and oilier foods. Eat more of the sweet, sour, and salty tastes. Avoid dry and cold/raw foods and drinks. Eat less pungent, bitter, and astringent tastes.

Symptoms of high/excess vata include, but are not limited to: constipation, insomnia, fatigue, emaciation, gas, bloating, discoloration of feces and urine, weakness in sensory perception, fear, mental

## Vata Pacifying Diet

anxiety, high levels of stress, feelings of coldness, and immune-deficiency disorders.

Vata is increased by: pungent, bitter, and astringent tastes and foods that are light, dry, and cold.

Vata can be decreased by: sweet, sour, and salty tastes and foods that are heavy, oily, and hot.

Here is a list of food group recommendations for the vata dosha.

- **Beans** – Reduce intake of beans, all of which increase vata, except for mung dhal. Mung beans can be taken frequently, if well cooked, with digestive herbs. Tempeh and tofu may be taken in moderation.
- **Oils** – All oils reduce vata. Sesame oil and ghee are best.
- **Vegetables** – Cooked beets, carrots, asparagus, onions, yams, and sweet potatoes are excellent for balancing vata. Celery, okra, zucchini, pumpkin, squash, green beans, mustard greens, and kale are also good options. For balancing vata, it is best to avoid raw vegetables. Try cooking with a little ghee, vegetable oil, or butter. Small amounts of vata-reducing spices can be used. Other vegetables may be taken in moderation if well cooked.

## Ayurvedic Nutrition

- **Spices** – Small quantities of black pepper, mustard seed, cumin, ginger, cinnamon, fennel, fenugreek, coriander, turmeric, basil, parsley, cilantro, black mustard seed, oregano, thyme, saffron, cinnamon, and cardamom are balancing for vata when cooked into meals. Moderate use of chillies and red pepper.
- **Grains** – Quinoa, basmati rice, oats, and millet are very good for vata balancing. Reduce intake of rye, barley, and corn.
- **Fruits** – Sweet and sour fruits are good for vata. This includes oranges, avocados, grapes, peaches, melons, fresh figs, papaya, berries, cherries, mangoes, sweet pineapple, apples, pears, persimmons, bananas, limes, lemons, and grapefruits.
- **Sweeteners** – Raw cane sugar, molasses, agave, jaggery, stevia, and honey are the best options for vata. All non-processed sweeteners are acceptable in moderation.
- **Nuts/Seeds** – All nuts and seeds benefit vata when taken in moderation.
- **Dairy** – As long as there is not lactose intolerance, all raw/organic/non-homogenized dairy products are good for vata, especially ghee, buttermilk, and yogurt. For ease of digestion, boil milk and drink it warm.

# Pitta Pacifying Diet

Pitta season is the hot and dry season. During this time, favor foods and drinks that are cooling. Eat foods of sweet, bitter, and astringent taste. Also include fresh, sweet fruits, and vegetables that grow during the pitta season. Eat less pungent, sour, and salty foods. Avoid yogurt, cheese, tomatoes, vinegars, and hot spices, as they all greatly increase pitta.

Symptoms of high/excess pitta include, but are not limited to: excessive hunger or thirst, burning sensation of skin, eyes or extremities, rashes, fevers, yellow discoloration, inflammatory diseases, anger, rage, hatred, jealousy, and impatience.

Pitta is increased by: pungent, sour, and salty tastes and foods that are hot, light, and dry.

Pitta can be decreased by: sweet, bitter, and astringent tastes and foods that are cold, heavy, and oily.

Here is a list of food group recommendations for the pitta dosha.

- **Beans** – Eat primarily adzuki, mung beans, and tempeh. All legumes are beneficial except lentils, as

*Ayurvedic Nutrition*

they can increase pitta. Avoid other soy products such as tofu.

- **Oils** – Butter, ghee, olive, sunflower, and coconut oils are best for pitta. Reduce use of almond, corn, and sesame oils, which increase pitta.
- **Vegetables** – Asparagus, cabbage, cucumber, peas, okra, zucchini, green beans, burdock root, turnips, parsnips, carrots, broccoli, cauliflower, sprouts, celery, and green leafy vegetables are balancing for pitta. Raw salads are great for pitta, especially in the summertime.
- **Spices** – Turmeric, coriander, cinnamon, fennel, mint, and cardamom are suitable for pitta. Chillies and cayenne, which aggravate pitta, should be avoided.
- **Grains** – Barley, oats, white basmati rice, and spelt are balancing for pitta. Brown rice, corn millet and rye intake should only be taken occasionally.
- **Fruits** – Sweet and astringent fruits like grapes, coconuts, cherries, avocado, melons, mangoes, pomegranates, prunes, oranges, plums, apples, pears, cranberries, and pineapples are good. Reduce intake of sour fruits, such as olives, under-ripe pineapple, or unripe bananas.

- **Sweeteners** – All natural sweeteners are good for pitta, but large quantities of honey should be avoided.
- **Nuts/Seeds** – Nuts should be avoided completely. Sunflower seeds can be taken in small quantities. Hempseeds can be taken on a regular basis.
- **Dairy** – As long as there is not lactose intolerance, non-homogenized raw/organic milk, butter, and ghee are good for pacifying pitta when used in moderation. Reduce the use of cheese, yogurt, sour cream, and cultured butter milk, as they aggravate pitta.

# Kapha Pacifying Diet

Kapha season is the wet and cool/rainy season. During kapha season, eat foods that are light and dry. Take warm food and drinks. Eat foods that are pungent, bitter, and astringent in taste. Avoid foods that are sweet, salty, or sour.

Symptoms of high/excess kapha include, but are not limited to: loss of appetite, heaviness in the body, cold hands and feet, swollen joints, cough with mucous, excessive sleeping, lethargy, dullness of mind, lack of concentration, and lack of inspiration.

*Ayurvedic Nutrition*

Kapha is increased by: sweet, sour, and salty tastes and foods that are heavy, oily, and cold.

Kapha can be decreased by: pungent, bitter, and astringent tastes and foods that are light, dry, and hot.

Here is a list of food group recommendations for the kapha dosha.

- **Beans** – All types of beans benefit kapha except kidney beans. Tofu should be reduced.
- **Oils** – Avoid large amounts of any oil. Almond and sunflower oils are acceptable in small amounts. Ghee can also be used in very small quantities with spices.
- **Vegetables** – Vegetables should be cooked and well spiced. All vegetables benefit kapha except cucumbers, eggplant, squash, spinach, sweet potato, and tomatoes. Especially good for kapha are radishes, turnips, dark leafy greens, celery, cabbage, and sprouts.
- **Spices** – Avoid salt, as it increases kapha. All spices benefit kapha, especially cayenne, black pepper, garlic, ginger, black mustard seed, and chillies, as these increase digestive fire.
- **Grains** – The grains that are most suitable for kapha are barley, quinoa, amaranth, buckwheat, rye, and

corn. Avoid wheat and rice. Millet should be taken only occasionally.

- **Fruits** – Eat lighter, more astringent fruits, including cranberries, apricots, berries, apples, and pomegranates. Dried fruits, such as raisins and prunes, are beneficial for kapha. Avoid heavy, very sweet or sour fruits, such as: grapes, bananas, figs, oranges, coconuts, pineapple, dates, and melons, as these increase kapha.
- **Sweeteners** – Honey and stevia are appropriate sweeteners for kapha. All other sweeteners should be avoided.
- **Nuts/Seeds** – Minimize nuts. Take pumpkin seeds, hemp seeds, and sunflower seeds in moderation.
- **Dairy** – Non-homogenized, raw, organic goat's milk and small quantities of spiced buttermilk can be taken occasionally. Kapha individuals should avoid dairy products as much as possible.

# Food Combining Chart

To encourage proper digestion and metabolism, it is best to keep food combinations simple. Mixing too many foods at once can create indigestion, bloating, gas, and uneasiness. Improper food combining causes foods to ferment in the stomach, thus smothering the

## *Ayurvedic Nutrition*

digestive fire and creating toxins. To ensure proper assimilation and to avoid feeling bloated and/or tired after meals, here are some points to consider regarding healthy food combinations:

| Don't Eat: | With: |
|---|---|
| Beans | fruit, cheese, eggs, fish, milk, meat, yogurt |
| Eggs | fruit, beans, cheese, fish, kichari, milk, meat, yogurt |
| Grains | Fruit |
| Fruit | any other food, except dates/almonds are okay |
| Hot Drinks | mangoes, cheese, fish, meat, starch, yogurt, large meals |
| Lemon | cucumbers, milk, tomatoes, yogurt |
| Melons | any other food, take only one type of melon at a time |
| Milk | bananas, cherries, melons, fruit, bread, fish, kichari, meat |
| Nightshades | cucumbers, dairy products |
| Radishes | bananas, raisins, milk |
| Tapioca/Yogurt | fruit, cheese, eggs, fish, hot drinks, meat, milk, nightshades |

# Acidity & Alkalinity

When the body is overly acidic, various symptoms can manifest, such as: fatigue, arthritis, indigestion, acid stomach, ulcers, headaches, insomnia, nervous tension, and osteoporosis. Chronic acidity also speeds up the aging process and causes tissue degeneration. A diet of predominantly fresh fruits and vegetables, with smaller amounts of whole grains and protein promotes alkalinity. Eating a diet based on meat, processed foods, or excessive carbohydrates creates acidity.

It is best to consume 80% alkaline-forming foods and 20% acid-forming foods.

## *Acidifying Foods*

**Fats & oils**
Avocado Oil
Canola Oil
Corn Oil
Flax Oil
Lard
Olive Oil
Safflower Oil
Sesame Oil
Sunflower Oil
Margarine
Hydrogenated Oil

**Grains**
Amaranth
Barley
Buckwheat
Corn
Oats (rolled)
Quinoa
Rice (all)
Rye
Spelt
Kamut
Wheat Flour
White Pasta

**Dairy**
Cheese
Milk
Butter
Eggs
Ice Cream

**Nuts & Butters**
Cashews
Brazil Nuts
Peanuts
Peanut Butter
Pecans

## Ayurvedic Nutrition

Tahini
Walnuts

**Other**
Distilled Vinegar
Wheat Germ
Potatoes
All Meat
Alcohol
Chemical Treated Water
Black Tea
Coffee
Carbonated Drinks
Canned Food
Microwaved Food
Chocolate

Iodized Salt

**Fruits**
Cranberries
Tomatoes
Smoothies with Dairy

**Drugs & Chemicals**
Chemicals
Drugs, Medicinal
Pesticides
Herbicides

**Beans & Legumes**
Black Beans

Chick Peas
Green Peas
Kidney Beans
Lentils
Lima Beans
Peanuts
Pinto Beans
Red Beans
Soy Beans
Soy Milk
White Beans
Rice Milk
Almond Milk

**Sweeteners**
White Sugar
Artificial Sugar

## Alkalinizing Foods

**Vegetables**
Garlic
Asparagus
Fermented Veggies
Beets
Broccoli
Brussel sprouts
Cabbage
Carrot
Cauliflower
Celery
Chard
Chlorella
Collard Greens
Cucumber
Kale
Lettuce
Mushrooms
Mustard Greens
Dandelions
Onions
Parsnips
Peas
Peppers
Pumpkin
Rutabaga
Sea Veggies
Spirulina
Sprouts
Squashes
Alfalfa
Barley Grass
Wheat Grass

**Fruits**
Apple
Apricot
Avocado
Banana
Cantaloupe
Cherries
Coconut
Dates/Figs
Grapes
Grapefruit
Lime
Honeydew Melon
Nectarine
Orange
Lemon
Peach

Pear
Pineapple
All Berries
Tangerine
Tropical Fruits
Watermelon

**Protein**
Almonds
Chestnuts
Flax Seeds
Pumpkin Seeds
Tempeh
Sunflower Seeds
Millet
Sprouted Seeds/Nuts

**Other**
Apple Cider
Vinegar
Bee Pollen
Probiotic
Cultures
Veggies Juices
Fresh Fruit Juice
Organic Milk
Mineral Water
Herbal Tea
Ginseng Tea
Bancha Tea
Kombucha

**Sweeteners**
Stevia

**Spices/Seasonings**
Cinnamon
Curry
Ginger
Mustard
Chilli Pepper
Sea Salt
Miso
Tamari
All Herbs

# Organic Food

*"Nature gives all of Her wealth to human beings.*
*Just as Nature is dedicated to helping us,*
*We too should be dedicated to helping Nature.*
*Only then can the harmony*
*between Nature and humanity be preserved."*

– Amma

For thousands of years, traditional agriculture used methods that respected nature's rhythms and utilized only substances that nature provided. Since the widespread use in farming of chemical fertilizers, pesticides, and herbicides, nature's balance has been upset, threatening the well being of not only of our external environment but also our internal environment.

Many farmers, having noticed these detrimental effects, have returned to using systems of organic agriculture that increase soil fertility and restore the harmony in nature. These systems include the addition of natural inputs such as compost, animal manures, and biodynamic preparations, as well as appropriate crop rotations. Plants grown in well-balanced, fertile soils are strong and healthy. They resist disease and pests in the same way a healthy, happy human resists disease.

Pesticides and chemical fertilizers are not necessary for farming. They are very destructive to soil life and to the health of plants. Residues of toxic pesticides and herbicides, when consumed through our food, accumulate in human body tissue. They also end up in waterways where their impact spreads widely throughout nature. Globally more than five billion pounds of pesticides are used every year.

In addition to being completely free from all chemicals, certified organic food is never irradiated after harvest. To become certified organic, produce must be grown in soil that is tested to be free from heavy-metal contamination. There is scientific evidence showing that the accumulation of the above-mentioned toxic substances in our bodies can lead to a wide variety of health problems, including; impaired immune function, cancer, allergies, autoimmune diseases, impaired fertility, and birth defects. Annually close to five million people worldwide suffer symptoms of pesticide poisoning. Furthermore, 10,000 people actually die from these poisons. Studies have shown the life span of conventional farmers is significantly shorter than that of organic farmers.

Currently many non-organic, commercial foods are genetically modified. Genetically modified organisms (GMOs) present a profound danger to humans as well as the ecosystem. Many species of animals, such as the monarch butterfly, are becoming extinct due to GMOs. For vegetarians, GMOs pose another problem, as they are frequently spliced from animal DNA. It is hypothesized by many experts that GMO food will eventually even alter human DNA. As GMOs are a recent creation, their long-term effects are unknown.

In India and other developing nations, western based GMO/pesticide companies are aggressively promoting extremely heavy use of chemicals for farming. This is leading to serious depletion of the soil and contamination of the water. Many insects are developing stronger resistence to pesticides, and sometimes even huge amounts of chemicals are ineffective. For this reason, many farmers have little or no yield, year after year. Having gone deeply in debt to these chemical companies, the farmers begin to feel hopeless. Unfortunately, large numbers of Indian farmers are committing suicide by drinking their pesticides. Amma has expressed concern about this issue, and is working to help the farmers and their families. When we choose organic, non-GMO foods, we can also do our part to try to end this tragic situation.

Certified organic food has much higher nutritional content than non-organic food, so the consumer gets more for their money. Many people also find that organic food tastes better. Organic food has higher life force (prana) than commercial food. Thus, it is clear that eating organic food is a primary step towards personal and global health.

# Water: The Fountain of Life

Water is essential for life. Our bodies are comprised of 80 percent water. The importance of maintaining internal hydration can be seen when comparing a piece of fresh fruit with a piece of dried fruit, the only difference being liquid. Without proper hydration, the body becomes dry, tough, and rigid. Water brings oxygen, nutrients, and life to our cells. Humans can live for a very long time without food, but can only survive for a short period without water. By the time we feel thirsty, our bodies are already very dehydrated. Making a habit of drinking water throughout the day will bring increased energy, vitality, and youthfulness.

Drinking at least 2-3 liters of water a day is very important to prevent dehydration. Thirst is often mistaken for hunger. Often, drinking water will eradicate false cravings for food. Without proper hydration, nutrients from food cannot be properly assimilated and toxins cannot be fully eliminated. Dehydration is one of the main causes of constipation.

Drink only pure spring water or filtered water. By adding EM-X ceramics or shaking the water bottle, the water becomes oxygenated. Thus, it experiences cellular re-structuring and more easily oxygenates blood and lymph while energizing the cells. Municipal water in the West often has been contaminated or processed with harmful chemicals that leach minerals from the bones and blood. These chemicals can lead to serious health problems, such as immune disorders, impaired neurological function, osteoporosis, nausea, and acidity. Also avoid drinking from very thin plastic water bottles, as the plastic contains carcinogenic substances that can contaminate the water.

# Activating & Revitalizing Food

Though it may not always be possible to access organic food and pure water, one way to revitalize depleted food is to chant mantras while cooking and before eating. In fact, it has even been scientifically proven that chanting mantras and praying physically regenerates food and water. Dr. Masaru Emoto, a scientist from Japan, has shown how mantras, gratitude, and loving intention instantly change the cellular structure of water. This is also the case with plants and food.

# Common Food Allergies

A surprising number of health issues arise from food allergies, intolerances, and sensitivities. The most common food allergies are to wheat, sugar, and dairy. Eliminating these foods alone, may remove many health issues. One way to test for food allergies/sensitivities is to remove the suspected allergen for a week to 10 days, then add it back into the diet and observe the effect that occurs in the body. Allopathic allergy tests and ayurvedic pulse diagnosis are also effective ways of determining allergies to foods. Sometimes food intolerances are dependant upon the quantity of the food ingested. For instance, some people may be fine eating small amounts of wheat, but after consuming large amounts, may develop indigestion.

Candidiasis is often associated with food allergies. It is an overgrowth of the yeast Candida Albicans, which is a normal part of the intestinal flora. This overgrowth can be induced by diets with refined sugars/carbohydrates and yeast, the use of antibiotics, alcohol, stress, and certain drugs such as the contraceptive pill. Candidiasis produces numerous intestinal, immunological, neurological, and other disorders. Symptoms can include tiredness, digestive problems, headaches, vaginal thrush, and immune weakness.

## *Wheat*

Half of all humans have sensitivities, allergies, or intolerances to wheat. Symptoms resulting from inability to assimilate wheat include: headache, bloated stomach, diarrhea, constipation, tiredness, rashes, arthritis, chest pains, depression, mood swings, eczema, dizziness, joint/muscle aches or pains, nausea, vomiting, heart palpitations, psoriasis, sneezing, cough, swollen throat or tongue, trouble going to sleep or waking up, runny nose, watery or itchy eyes, and lack of concentration.

Diseases/ailments that have been found to be directly related to wheat sensitivities/allergies include: arthritis, arteriosclerosis, rheumatism, immune disorders, multiple sclerosis, Alzheimer's, Parkinson's, IBS, colon cancer, uterine cancer, breast cancer, lymphoma, heart disease, Crohn's disease, gout, high blood pressure, and heartburn.

For those who do not have a wheat sensitivity or Candidiasis, it is highly nutritive. It is one of the most strengthening of all grains. It helps build muscle tissue and gives energy for physical exertion. The best way to consume wheat is sprouted or as chapattis. It helps to alleviate high vata, as it calms the mind and strengthens the heart. It is also excellent for countering insomnia. As it is made of mostly the earth element (kapha), those who have excessive kapha should minimize wheat consumption. Wheat intake should be limited when there are toxins present in the body or when experiencing colds or congestion.

## *Alternatives to Wheat*

There are now many breads, such as spelt and ragi (millet), that are wheat-free or gluten-free. Spelt and rice noodles make wonderful pasta alternatives. Many grains such as oats, quinoa, etc. are hearty nutritive staples. In India, dosa, ootapam, and idly are good wheat-free options.

## *Sugar*

Intolerance to processed sugar is very common, and manifests as chronic tiredness, depression, mood swings, behavioral and learning disorders, poor concentration, intestinal disturbances, and headaches. People often crave or become addicted to the foods to which they are intolerant. This often happens with sugar; and results in binge eating.

Processed sugar affects our health in other ways, apart from causing intolerance reactions. It lacks significant nutritional value. It is a source of energy, but lacks any vitamins or minerals. In fact, to digest and utilize white sugar, the body must use up its own vitamins, minerals, and nutrients, especially potassium, magnesium, calcium, and B vitamins. This can lead to nutrient deficiencies when large amounts of processed sugar are consumed. Significant consumption of processed sugar is associated with the development of obesity, diabetes, hypertension, and cardiovascular disease. There is a global epidemic of these diseases, and even people at a young age are being affected. It also causes tooth decay. Consuming large amounts of processed sugar can have a negative effect on the intestinal flora, causing intestinal dysbiosis, such as Candidiasis. For centuries, naturopaths have recognized the connection between healthy intestines and a healthy body, which is now being now scientifically verified. A direct link between healthy intestinal flora and immune function has been established.

Most people consume far more processed sugar than the body can use for energy. In America, an average of 130 pounds of processed sugar is consumed per year per person. This translates to 1/3 of a pound of processed sugars a day per person. Many times, consumers are unaware of the large amounts of processed sugar hidden in packaged foods.

## *Alternatives to White Sugar*

In the ayurvedic tradition, unprocessed cane sugar is used as a tonic, to rejuvenate and counteract debility. It is often included as part of medicinal formulas, such as chayawanprash.

**Jaggery:** High quality jaggery is an excellent substitute, as it is filled with many digestible minerals and doesn't spike blood-sugar levels like white sugar. It is also much easier on the liver and spleen.

**Stevia:** Stevia is the perfect sweetener, as it has beneficial nutrients; and tests are now showing that it even helps to correct diabetes by balancing blood-sugar levels.

**Fruit:** Natural and extracted fruit sugars are also much better choices than white sugar. However, these do cause a large spike in blood-sugar levels, so those who have high Candida levels should be careful not to consume them in excess.

**Sucanat/Turbinado:** This is pure unrefined cane sugar. High quality sucanat is filled with minerals and can be beneficial for the liver/spleen/pancreas. Again, those with high Candida levels or sugar sensitivities should minimize all sugars.

**Date Sugar/Blackstrap Molassas:** Both are filled with valuable nutrients such as iron.

**Honey/Agave Nectar:** Both of these are filled with numerous nutrients and increase assimilation. Ayurveda says that honey should never be cooked. Cooked honey transforms into a sticky glue-like substance that adheres to mucous membranes and clogs the gross and subtle channels, producing toxins. Uncooked honey is considered to be amrita (nectar).

Synthetic sweeteners are not good sugar substitutes. In laboratory tests, they have proven to be carcinogenic neurotoxins.

## *Milk /Dairy*

Lactose intolerance affects at least one out of every five people. Lactose intolerance creates similar conditions as wheat and sugar intolerance. Unless one is lactose intolerant, raw, organic, non-homogenized, non-pasteurized milk can provide many healthy benefits. It is the processing of the milk, not the milk itself, that leads to imbalance in the human body.

Traditionally in ayurveda, milk was considered a complete and perfect food. It was used by the yogis and rishis daily to increase health. Unfortunately, these days, pure quality milk is not readily available. In days past, cows roamed freely, breathing fresh air, grazing on pure grass, absorbing pure sunlight, and being treated with love and respect.

Today, the majority of dairy cows spend their lives locked in confined spaces, being pumped full or hormones and antibiotics, so that they will grow bigger and produce more milk. When they can no longer produce, most commercial dairy cows are sent to the slaughterhouse.

Many companies are now using extremely large quantities of growth hormones and antibiotics on their cows, and some even promote this as a good selling point. This reflects a major lack of understanding. Commercial dairy consumption is believed to contribute to the human body's increasing resistance to antibiotics and disturbance of the intestinal flora. The effects of ingested growth hormones are not fully understood. There is evidence to suggest that they

## Ayurvedic Nutrition

adversely affect the immune, hormonal, and nervous systems. They may also be associated with increased incidences of certain cancers, especially breast cancer.

Pasteurization is a sterilization process in which products are heated to high temperatures to destroy potentially harmful bacteria. Homogenization acts

## Common Food Allergies

as a preservative and extends shelf life. In this process valuable vitamins are lost, and there are changes to the milk's chemical structure. Ayurveda explains that, after pasteurization, enzymes in the milk are lost. This results in malabsorbtion and an increase in toxins in the colon.

Homogenization was introduced in 1932. It is a process where under the pressure of 4,000 pounds per square inch, at 600 feet per second, milk is passed through very fine filters and pipes. This breaks up the fat cells and puts them into a fine suspension. In this form, the body is unable to assimilate or utilize the milk properly. Fat is deposited in arterial walls, forming atherosclerotic plaque. As atherosclerosis progresses, it can lead to heart attacks and strokes. Studies show that undigested molecules from homogenized milk may also contribute to prostate enlargement and cancer. Skim milk and low-fat milk are no different. Pasteurization and homogenization still change milk's chemical structure.

As a result of all these factors, commercial dairy products can cause numerous problems including acidity, cramping, nausea, diarrhea, flatulence, bloating, nasal blockages, nasal mucous, mucoidal plaque in the colon, and a variety of other symptoms. Therefore, the healthiest way to ingest dairy is to consume organic, non-homogenized, non-pasteurized milk products from cows that have been treated with love.

## *Healthy Forms of Dairy & Dairy Alternatives*

Raw milk is much easier to digest than homogenized dairy. It nurtures the tissues, bones, and hair. One great alternative to using homogenized milk is purchasing hormone/antibiotic-free cow, goat, or sheep milk and boiling it for a minute on your own to sterilize it without excessively destroying nutrients. Raw milk can also be turned into a healthier version of cheese and yogurt. One possible alternative for people with lactose intolerance is goat and sheep dairy products. These contain much lower amounts of lactose. When consumed in moderation, they are often digested more easily than cow dairy.

Before homogenization was created, many cultures used milk products as staple foods. Taking milk in unadulterated forms is much more beneficial for the body. However, according to ayurveda, the use of dairy products should be varied according to one's dosha (please see the doshic diet sections earlier in this book).

## Common Food Allergies

Ghee is unsalted butter that has been cooked so that all impurities are removed. It can be stored without refrigeration. It nourishes all the dhatus (tissues), helps improve assimilation and absorption, nourishes the nervous system, and lubricates joints and muscles. It also increases digestive enzymes and is beneficial for the liver. It is a healthy form of fat as it does not increase total cholesterol and helps build HDL (beneficial cholesterol). Unlike most oils, ghee can be cooked for a long time without creating free radicals. Ghee can be used for cooking. It is also commonly used as a carrier for ayurvedic medicines, as it helps deliver nutrients deeply into the body.

Milk alternatives are increasingly available throughout the world. Rice milk, hemp milk, almond milk, oat milk, and hazelnut milk are being made as dairy alternatives. These are excellent choices for those with lactose intolerance. Soy milk, though more common than other dairy alternatives, should be used with caution. Many people also have soy sensitivity and may have difficulty digesting soy products. Yogurt and cheese alternatives are also available.

*Ayurvedic Nutrition*

# What's That on Your Plate?

As disease and sickness are rapidly increasing, many people are feeling the urgency to make significant dietary changes. There are numerous "foods" that we as a society consume on a daily basis that are rapidly destroying our health—physically, mentally, emotionally, and spiritually. The purpose of this section is to increase awareness so that you can make an educated choice about the fuel (food) you put into your vehicle (body).

Here is a list of items that greatly decrease our health and longevity:

- Processed Salt
- Caffeine
- Refined Foods
- Fatty Foods
- Fried Food
- Fiber-less Food
- Chemical Additives/Preservatives
- Soda/Processed Carbonated Drinks
- Alcohol

**Salt:** Ayurveda states that salt increases pitta and kapha, while decreasing vata. Small amounts of salt increase appetite and improve flavor. In excess, salt aggravates the doshas, overheats the nerves, and weakens digestion. In general, most people consume excessive amounts of processed salt, in the form of inorganic sodium chloride. Salt, like sugar, is hidden in many processed foods. It is highly addictive, and in excess, causes kapha related disorders such as: high blood pressure, weakening of the bones, weakened kidneys, water retention, hardening of arteries, and bronchial/lung weakness.

Healthy salts include organic sea salt, rock salt, liquid amino acids, and Himalayan salt, all of which contain water-soluble minerals in an easily assimilated form. Seaweeds are an excellent processed salt alternative, full of trace and ionic minerals. They add a salty taste to the diet while alkalinizing, oxygenating, and mineralizing the blood and body. Seaweeds also help to draw heavy metals and chemicals out of the body. All seaweeds are beneficial; dulse, arame, hijiki, wakame, and kombu are found in most health food stores and Asian markets. Another good alternative is miso, which adds a salty flavor to food while supporting digestion and alkalinizing the body.

**Caffeine:** Caffeine is contained in tea, coffee, chocolate, and cola. Many people have intolerance to caf-

*Ayurvedic Nutrition*

feine and become addicted to it. Common symptoms of this include: chronic tiredness, hyper-tension, palpitations, stress, anxiety, mood swings, irritability, anger, insomnia, nausea, indigestion, constipation, diarrhea, and liver/kidney problems. It is a stimulant, and chronic use often depletes the body's reserves, weakening and stressing the adrenal glands, nervous system, and immune system. Excessive consumption can lead to osteoporosis and nutritional deficiencies. It is best avoided, especially in people with health problems or sensitive constitutions.

Coffee causes many more problems than tea, because of higher caffeine content and the presence of other active substances, such as methyl-xanthine, which can irritate the stomach lining and destroy beneficial bacteria. High quality black tea, taken in moderation, may be beneficial for certain conditions. Excessive use, however, can inhibit the assimilation of iron, calcium, and zinc from food, especially if consumed during meals. Black tea should especially be avoided by those with excess vata/pitta conditions such as: weakened nervous systems, liver problems, insomnia, ADD/ADHD, and hyper-acidity.

There are several substitutes that can be made for coffee and black tea. Green tea is high in antioxidants, and has been found to reduce the incidence of certain infections and cancers. Yerba Mate, an herbal tea from South America, is an excellent substitute. Although it contains some caffeine, it doesn't aggravate the nervous system or digestive system the way coffee does. It contains 24 vitamins and minerals, 15 amino acids, abundant antioxidants, and chlorophyll. Grain coffee, roasted chicory, dandelion root, etc. may also be used as a substitute for the taste of coffee and contain no caffeine. Many natural herbal teas have numerous health benefits and are caffeine free.

A great alternative to chocolate is cacao, or chocolate in its raw, unprocessed form. Cacao is the seed of a fruit of a tree called Theobroma, which literally means "the food of the gods." Cacao beans contain no sugar and are extremely full of nutrients. When cacao is processed into chocolate with added dairy and sugar, it loses many of its healthy properties. In its raw form, cacao has abundant antioxidants and B vitamins, as well as magnesium, which balances brain chemistry and builds strong bones. While chocolate contains substantially less caffeine than coffee, cacao contains even more subtle amounts. Research is now showing that raw cacao has mood-elevating properties.

## Ayurvedic Nutrition

**Refined Foods:** Refined foods such as bleached flours and polished rice are deficient in minerals and vitamins. When they are de-husked, many nutrients are lost. Use of these products depletes B-vitamins from the body, resulting in fatigue. They also weaken bones, increase blood-sugar levels, and cause constipation due to lack of fibrous content. Un-refined, un-processed, whole foods are always a more nurturing option.

**Fatty Foods:** The human body requires a certain amount of good fats to maintain a healthy balance. Fats give the body twice the energy of carbohydrates, and are required for certain vitamin absorption (Vitamins A, D, E, K). Essential fatty acids (EFA's) are necessary for health. Saturated fats are derived from animal fats and coconut. An excessive intake of animal fats can cause elevated cholesterol levels, heart disease, vascular disease, and obesity. Poly-unsaturated fats are vegetable-derived fats and are beneficial in proper amounts. In excess, they can cause the same problems as saturated fats. Of these, mono-saturated fats are considered the healthiest.

Hydrogenated fats/trans -fatty acids are oils which have been modified to prolong shelf life. They are solid at room temperature, and are often found in margarine, processed foods, and fried foods. They are quite toxic because they increase cholesterol more significantly than saturated fats and generate free radicals in the body. Free radicals are unstable oxygen molecules along with unpaired electrons. These become reactive and cause havoc in our bodies by severely damaging our cell structure, its membranes, fat, proteins, the DNA and RNA. They are major contributors to cancer, heart disease, arthritis, rheumatism, gout, brain degeneration, Parkinson's, Alzheimer's, and senility. Free radical damage accelerates the body's aging process. Free radicals are somewhat counteracted with whole fresh fruits, herbs, and vegetables.

The healthiest fats to use are ghee, high-quality vegetable oils, and oils high in EFA's, such as hemp seed, flax, and evening primrose oils. Those with weak digestive fire, high cholesterol, or kapha-related disorders should limit all oil consumption.

**Fried Food:** Most fried food is cooked with very poor-quality oils, and is cooked at very high temperatures. The oils used for frying are often hydrogenated, and are very damaging to the body, as explained previously. Fried foods also increase obesity and total cholesterol levels. This can lead to heart attacks and strokes. Frying foods destroys nutrients, and creates indigestion, constipation, stomach acidity, and numerous other digestive disorders. It is best to avoid consumption of fried food. Frying with canola, safflower, soy or peanut oil should especially be avoided, as they become rancid/carcinogenic more quickly than other oils. If frying, it is best to use ghee, because it does not undergo any toxic changes when heated.

**Fiber-less Food:** Dietary fiber or roughage is a necessity in the human diet. Dietary fiber lowers cholesterol, controls blood-sugar levels, lowers blood pressure, prevents constipation, helps in weight reduction, and decreases toxicity in the body. The RDA of daily dietary fiber in the US is about 30-40g.

>  **Low Fiber:** White bread, clear soups, cake, potato chips, noodles, fruit juice, all types of animal products, processed sugar, eggs, pizza, ice cream, pastries, white rice, white flour, milk, and fats.
> **High fiber:** Whole grains, wheat (especially sprouted), oats, corn, barley, millet, quinoa, basmati rice, brown rice, all beans, almost all vegetables, and most fruits.

**Chemical Additives/Preservatives:** Chemical additives are prevalent in most mainstream foods. Chemical additives are used in virtually all refined, non-organic foods as preservatives, buffers, emulsifiers, neutralizing agents, sequestering agents, stabilizers, anti-caking agents, flavoring, and coloring. They have a wide range of known potential negative effects on the body, including; allergies, asthma, anaphylaxis, migraines, behavioral disorders, ADD/ADHD, gastrointestinal imbalance, bloating, diarrhea, and cancer.

Main chemical additives like Butylated Hydroxy Anisole (BHA) and Butylated Hydroxy Toluene (BHT) are anti-oxygenating agents that produce toxins in the nervous and immune systems. Red No. 2, 40, and Yellow No. 5 are carcinogenic coloring agents. MSG, sometimes called "Chinese salt," is now being disguised on labels in generic terms such as "flavors" or even "natural flavors." MSG has even caused fatalities associated with sudden anaphylaxis. For cultivating good health, it is best to choose non-processed, chemical free foods.

**Soda/Processed Carbonated Drinks:** Soda and processed carbonated drinks are often loaded with caffeine and processed sugar. The average American drinks an estimated 56 gallons of soft drinks each year. Fifty-six percent of American 8-year-olds down soft drinks daily, and a third of teenage boys drink at least three cans of soda pop per day. A single 12 ounce can of soda contains up to twelve teaspoons of sugar.

Even diet/caffeine-free sodas can be filled with toxic ingredients. Phosphoric acid and aspartame are common components of soda. Phosphoric acid may interfere with the body's ability to use calcium, which can lead to osteoporosis and softening of the teeth and bones. Phosphoric acid also neutralizes the hydrochloric acid in your stomach, which can interfere with digestion, making it difficult to utilize nutrients. A 1994 Harvard study of bone fractures in teenage athletes found a strong association between cola soda consumption and bone fractures in 14-year-old girls. The girls who drank cola were about five times more likely to suffer bone fractures than girls who didn't consume soda pop.

Aspartame is a chemical commonly used as a sugar substitute in diet soda. There are over 92 different health side effects associated with aspartame consumption including brain tumors, birth defects, diabetes, emotional disorders and epilepsy/seizures.

Further, when aspartame is stored for long periods of time or kept in warm areas it changes to methanol, an alcohol that converts to formaldehyde and formic acid, which are known carcinogens.

Researchers have found that just two cans of soda can suppress immune function for up to five hours. Scientific studies have shown how as few as one or two soft drinks a day can significantly increase one's risk for numerous health problems, such as; obesity, diabetes, tooth decay, osteoporosis, insomnia, ADD/ADHD, caffeine dependence, nutritional deficiencies, heart disease, and many neurological disorders.

Drinking pure water is the optimal form of liquid intake. Organic food companies are now making natural cola/soft drinks with herbal extracts and unprocessed sweeteners. Juices and herbal teas are also good replacements for heavily processed sodas.

**Alcohol:** Ayurveda uses some forms of alcohol as a base for extracting the medicinal properties from herbs. However, regular consumption of alcohol for recreation purposes is not recommended because it aggravates all three doshas. Alcohol is highly addictive, and in excess acts as a depressant. It is extremely harmful to the nervous system, causing peripheral neuropathy and dementia. It depletes B-vitamins, damages liver cells, leads to cirrhosis and diabetes, creates gastritis and inflammation of the stomach by irritating the mucous membranes, and increases Candida overgrowth. It raises blood pressure, lowers immunity, and can lead to decreased bone mass. The after effects of excessive alcohol consumption are fatigue, headache, nausea, dehydration, and constipation.

We have been blessed with a precious human body. Let us all nurture our bodies with wholesome foods, so we are able to serve, love, and reach our life's potential.

# Dharmic Dining

*"Diet has a great deal of influence on our character. Children, you should take care to eat only simple, fresh, vegetarian food (sattvic food). The nature of the mind is determined by the subtle essence of the food we eat. Pure food creates a pure mind. Without forsaking the taste of the tongue, the taste of the heart cannot be enjoyed."*

– Amma

*Dharmic Dining*

Saving the lives of animals may save your own life. There is extensive evidence that vegetarian/vegan diets are by far the healthiest diets. Scientific research is now proving that the overconsumption of cholesterol and saturated fats in animal products leads to heart disease and numerous forms of cancers. The consumption of animal products also leads to obesity, diabetes, hypertension, arthritis, gout, kidney stones, and a vast number of other diseases. In addition, modern-day factory farming methods use excessive amounts of hormones, antibiotics, chemical fertilizers, and drugs to increase their output and profits. Commercial animal products contain high levels of herbicides and pesticides. When humans consume animal products, these poisons enter directly into the body and cause toxicity.

Since the 1960s, scientists have suspected that a meat-based diet is related to the development of arteriosclerosis and heart disease. As early as 1961, a study published in the *Journal of the American Medical Association* reported: "Ninety to 97 percent of heart disease can be prevented by a vegetarian diet." Since that time, several well-organized studies have scientifically shown that, after tobacco and alcohol, the consumption of meat is the greatest single cause of mortality in Europe, the United States, Australia, and other affluent areas of the world.

The human body is unable to deal with excessive amounts of animal fat and cholesterol, which accumulate on the inner walls of the arteries, constrict the flow of blood to the heart, and can lead to high blood pressure, heart disease, and strokes. Research during the past 20 years also strongly suggests a link between meat-eating and cancer of the colon, rectum, breast, and uterus. An article in *The Lancet*, a UK-based medical journal, reported, "People living in the areas with a high-recorded incidence of carcinoma of the colon tend to live on diets containing large amounts of fat and animal protein; whereas those who live in areas with a low incidence live on largely vegetarian diets with little fat or animal matter."

Why do meat-eaters seem more prone to these diseases? One reason given by biologists and nutritionists is that the human intestinal tract is simply not suited for digesting meat. Flesh-eating animals have short intestinal tracts, three times the length of the body, to pass rapidly decaying toxin-producing meat out of the body quickly. Since plant foods decay more slowly than meat, plant-eaters have intestines at least six times the length of the body. Humans have the long intestinal tract of an herbivore.

Another concerning issue with meat is that of chemical contamination. As soon as an animal is slaughtered, its flesh begins to putrefy, and after several days it turns a sickly gray-green. The meat industry masks this discoloration by adding nitrites, nitrates, and other preservatives to give the meat a bright red color. But research now shows most of these preservatives to be carcinogenic. Further exacerbating the problem are the massive amount of chemicals fed to livestock. Gary and Steven Null, in their book *Poisons in Your Body* show us something that ought to make anyone think twice before buying another steak or ham. "The animals are kept alive and fattened by continuous administration of tranquilizers, hormones, antibiotics, and 2,700 other drugs. The process starts even before birth and continues long after death. Although these drugs will still be present in the meat when you eat it, the law does not require that they be listed on the package."

As for the protein question, Dr. Paavo Airo, a leading authority on nutrition and natural biology, has this to say: "The official daily recommendation for protein has gone down from the 150 grams recommended

20 years ago to only 45 grams today. Why? Because reliable worldwide research has shown that we do not need so much protein, that the actual daily need is only 35 to 45 grams. Protein consumed in excess of the daily need is not only wasted, but actually can cause harm to the body, as it strains to digest it. In order to obtain 45 grams of protein a day from your diet you do not have to eat meat; you can get it easily from a 100 percent vegetarian diet of a variety of grains, lentils, nuts, vegetables, and fruits."

One of ayurveda's foundational principles is ahimsa (non-violence). Killing animals for food is not only violence to the animal but harms the environment and all the hungry people in the world. It promotes ongoing suffering. A surprising amount of people don't consider fish to be meat. Fish are, in fact, animals and can feel suffering as they are being killed. When an animal is killed, it releases fear hormones and other toxins into its body, which are later ingested and absorbed into the meat-eater's body. That negative emotional vibration then enters into the human's consciousness. In addition, meat is dead. It is completely void of prana (life force). As such, according to ayurveda, meat creates tamas (dullness/darkness) in the mind and body.

*Dharmic Dining*

Albert Einstein said, "Our task must be to free ourselves, by widening our circle of compassion to embrace all living creatures and the whole of nature and its beauty. Nothing will benefit human health and increase our chances of survival for life on earth as much as the evolution to a vegetarian diet."

In the ancient Indian epic *Mahabharata*, there are numerous statements against killing animals. "Who can be more cruel and selfish than he who augments his flesh by eating the flesh of innocent animals? Those who desire to possess good memory, beauty, long life with perfect health, and physical, moral, and spiritual strength should abstain from animal food."

In addition to the concerns of health and ethics, the vegetarian and vegan lifestyle has a higher, spiritual dimension that can help us develop our natural appreciation and love of God.

# Ending World Hunger

*"One who has faith and devotion to God, which in turn stems from one's innate innocence, beholds God in everything, in every tree and animal, in every aspect of Nature. This attitude enables one to live in harmony and in tune with Nature. It is wrong to waste due to our lack of care and attention. Every object has been created to be used; every object in creation has a definite purpose."*

– Amma

Many people become vegetarian for environmental or socio-economic reasons. Our Mother Earth has limited resources that must be used wisely and consciously. Eating a vegetarian diet is one of the best ways to conserve earth's resources and maintain a balanced economy. Meat feeds few at the expense of many. For the sake of producing meat, grain that could feed people feeds livestock instead.

According to information compiled by the United States Department of Agriculture, more than 90 percent of all the grain produced in America goes to feed livestock – cows, pigs, sheep, and chickens – that wind up on dinner tables. Yet the process of using grain to produce meat is incredibly wasteful. Their figures show that for every 16 pounds of grain fed to cattle, we get back only one pound of meat.

In *Diet for a Small Planet*, Frances Moore Lappe asks us to imagine ourselves sitting down to an eight-ounce steak. "Then imagine the room filled with 45 to 50 people with empty bowls in front of them. For the 'feed cost' of your steak, each of their bowls could be filled with a full cup of cooked cereal grains."

Affluent nations not only waste their own grains to feed livestock, but also use protein-rich plant foods from poor nations. Dr. George Borgstrom, an authority on the geography of food, estimates that more than one third of Africa's nut crop (which is very high in protein) ends up in the stomachs of cattle and poultry in Western European cuisine.

In underdeveloped countries, a person consumes an average of 400 pounds of grain a year. In contrast, says world food authority Lester Brown, the average meat eater goes through 2,000 pounds of grain a year, by first feeding almost 90 percent of it to animals for meat. The average meat-eater, Brown says, uses five times the food resources of the average vegetarian. Facts such as these have led food experts to point out that the world-hunger problem is unnecessary. Even now, we are already producing more than enough food for everyone on the planet. Unfortunately, we are allocating it wastefully. Harvard nutritionist Jean Mayer estimates that bringing down meat production by only 10 percent would release enough grain to feed 60 million people.

# Eating Up Resources

*"Only after the last tree has been cut down,*
*only after the last river has been poisoned,*
*only after the last fish has been caught,*
*only then will one find that money cannot be eaten."*
Cree Prophecy

• One acre of land can produce 20,000 pounds of potatoes. The same amount of land can only make 165 pounds of meat.
• It takes 16 pounds of grain to produce one pound of meat.

## Eating Up Resources

- More than half of the harvested agriculture acreage goes to feed livestock.
- It requires 3 ½ acres of land to support a meat-centered diet, 1 ½ acres of land to support a lacto-ovo vegetarian diet, and 1/6th of an acre to support a vegan diet.
- It takes approximately 2,500 gallons of water to produce a single pound of meat. It takes 4,000 gallons of water to provide a day's amount of food per person on a meat-based diet. It takes 1,200 gallons of water for a person on a lacto-ovo vegetarian diet, and 300 gallons of water for a vegan diet.
- Developing nations predominantly use their land to raise beef for wealthier nations instead of utilizing that land for sustainable agriculture practices.
- In order to support cattle grazing, South and Central America are destroying their rainforests. These rainforests contain close to half of all the species on Earth, including thousands of medicinal plants. More than a thousand species a year are becoming extinct and most of these are from the rainforest or tropical settings used for the meat industry. This practice is also rapidly causing the displacement of indigenous peoples who have been living in harmony in these environments for thousands of years. Additionally, this is contributing to global warming.

- For each acre of forest land that is cleared for human purposes, seven acres of forest is cleared for growing livestock feed. This policy is very rapidly destroying the few remaining forests.
- Topsoil is the dark, rich soil that supplies the nutrients to the food we grow. It takes more than 500 years to make one inch of topsoil. This soil is rapidly vanishing due to clear cutting of forests for cattle grazing.
- Water is being contaminated by chemically based farming methods used to raise animals. Because of such poisoning of our freshwater resources, we are quickly running out of clean drinking water.

# Vitamins & Nutrients

Many people have been conditioned to believe that they can only get enough protein and essential vitamins, minerals and nutrients by eating meat and animal products. Actually, numerous food sources offer an array of adequate nutrition choices. Mother Nature provides an abundance of nourishing plant sources.

**Protein:** The combination of grains and legumes gives the complete range of amino acids necessary to synthesize any protein. In ayurveda, kichari is a traditional food that combines basmati rice and mung dhal to create a complete protein. Protein can also be obtained through hemp seeds, grains, grain products, nuts, seeds, beans, lentils, cabbage, beet greens, organic dairy, spirulina, and all green superfoods. Ragi (black millet) and quinoa are particularly full of protein. Plants, especially green leafy vegetables, micro algae, and sea vegetables contain a large amount of amino acids, the building blocks of protein. Hemp and rice protein powders are easily assimilated forms of concentrated protein. Soya products also contain protein. However, soya products should be used with caution, as they are often difficult to digest due to GMOs and over-processing. Tempeh is a form of soya that people often find to be more easily digestible. Eggs are not generally recommended in ayurveda for karmic reasons and because they aggravate pitta and kapha. They also increase cholesterol levels and weaken digestive fire. Nearly all non-organic commercial eggs are factory farmed. If you choose to use eggs, please try to avoid using factory farmed eggs, as they come from chickens that have undergone intense suffering.

**B-12:** B-12 is responsible for the formation of red blood cells and the maintenance of a healthy nervous system. This is the one vitamin that vegetarians/vegans are frequently lacking, as it is found in high concentrations in meat. It can also be obtained from eating seaweeds, micro algae/spirulina, and soya. Also, most vegetarian/vegan foods on the consumer market are fortified with B-12. Yeast/nutritional flakes, veggieburgers/-dogs, veggie meats, grains, cereals, rice/hemp/almond milks all provide sufficient B-12.

**Vitamin D:** Vitamin D regulates absorption and excretion of calcium, especially when calcium levels are low. Vitamin D is only present in fish, eggs, and dairy in small amounts. It is strongly concentrated in nutritional flakes. Like B-12, most vegetarian/vegan food products are fortified with enough Vitamin D. The highest source of Vitamin D comes from the sun and 10-15 minutes in the early morning or late afternoon sun two to three times a week is adequate to supply enough Vitamin D.

**Calcium:** Calcium is responsible for the growth and maintenance of bones, hair, nails, skin, and joints. There is a major misconception that the best source of calcium is milk and dairy products. Studies now suggest that the unstable proteins from homogenized milk may actually cause minerals, including calcium, to leach out of the body. A 12-year Harvard University study involving 78,000 females drinking two glasses of pasteurized/homogenized milk a day, showed significantly higher risk of hip and bone fracture, compared to those who drank one or no glasses of milk per day. This implies that homogenized milk does not protect against bone loss. Additionally, in countries where dairy is not a dietary staple, there is significantly less osteoporosis. Sesame seeds, especially in the form of black tahini, have the highest concentration of calcium. Absorbable plant-based sources of calcium include: green leafy vegetables, dried fruit, seeds, nuts, ragi (black millet), as well as grain milks/cereals/etc. that are fortified with calcium.

**Iron:** Iron deficiency can result in pale skin, brittle fingernails, fatigue, weakness of blood/bones, shortness of breath, menstrual disorders, body-temperature fluctuation, loss of appetite, apathy, and anemia. Homogenized dairy products, coffee, processed/artificial sugar, and black tea all inhibit the assimilation of iron. Vitamin C increases the absorbability of iron. Good sources of iron include: all beans, pumpkin seeds, blackstrap molasses, dates, raisins, grains, and seaweeds.

It is ideal to meet nutritional needs through eating pure, whole foods. In some situations, when this is not possible, supplements may be required. All of the vitamins and minerals listed above can be found in supplement form as well. It is important to be aware that many supplements on the market contain binders and fillers that actually inhibit the absorption of vitamins and minerals. Therefore, it is important to check the ingredient sources and is sometimes necessary to take more than the suggested daily dose on the bottles. Liquid minerals and vitamins are the most easily assimilated form as they can enter directly into the bloodstream. Vegetarians may also want to avoid using supplements that contain gelatin, as it is made from the hooves of animals such as pigs and horses.

# Body Care & Household Cleaning Products

The skin is the largest organ in the body and readily absorbs many substances that come into contact with it. Body-care product ingredients, once absorbed

## Body Care & Household Cleaning Products

through our skin, move directly into the lymph and blood. From here they make their way to the organs, especially the liver. Toxic chemicals, preservatives, processed sugar, and other artificial ingredients are often hidden in many commercial body-care products. Household cleaners are usually filled with harmful chemicals that are absorbed not only through the skin, but also come into the body through the respiratory system when we breathe their vapors. For optimum health, it is wise to use completely natural body-care and household-cleaning products.

Some ingredients labeled "derived from natural sources" may contain harmful chemicals that are not produced by nature but form as a result of the refinement process. The labels on many cosmetic, skin-care, and household-cleaning products contain ingredient names written in the language of chemistry. Most common brands of "natural" or "herbal" shampoos and cleansers still use these harmful chemicals as their main active ingredient. Take time to read labels and try to avoid these dangerous ingredients, which are commonly found in toothpastes, shampoos, conditioners, deodorants, soaps, lotions, sunscreens, make-up, and cleaning products, and are also sometimes found in food.

## Ayurvedic Nutrition

**Acetone** is a neurotoxin, a strong skin/eye irritant, and causes adverse effects on the respiratory and nervous systems.

**Aluminum** is a common ingredient in many antiperspirants, and can even be present in food products such as baking powder. It increases lymph toxicity and is believed to be a contributing factor in breast cancer. Aluminum is also directly related to neurological deterioration and diseases such as Alzheimer's and Parkinson's.

**Artificial colors** have been shown to cause cancer when applied to the skin. Often, artificial colors contain heavy-metal impurities, including arsenic and lead, which are carcinogenic.

**Butylated hydroxianisole** (BHA)/**Butylated hydroxytoluene** (BHT), found in both food and body-care products, are carcinogens capable of corroding metal. They can cause dermatitis and skin/eye irritation.

**Cocamide DEA** or **MEA** and **Lauramide DEA** are skin/eye irritants. Repeated skin applications of DEA-based detergents are shown to result in a major increase in the incidence of liver and kidney cancers.

**Formaldehyde** is used in thousands of cosmetics and is known to cause eye, nose, and throat irritation, coughing, asthma attacks, shortness of breath, nausea, vomiting, skin rashes, nosebleeds, headaches, and dizziness. It is known to cause serious weakening of the immune system.

**Fragrances** is a term that refers to a wide range of ingredients. Many of these "fragrances" cause birth defects, reproductive impairments, and liver damage in lab animals. Manufacturers are not required to list the ingredients used in "fragrance," but common ingredients also include methylene chloride, toluene, methyl ethyl ketone, methyl isobutyl ketone, ethyl alcohol, and benzyl chloride, all of which are hazardous and can cause allergic reactions.

**Mineral oil**, **petrolatum**, **paraffin wax/oil**, **liquidum paraffinum**, and **parabens** (methyl, propyl, butyl) are petroleum by-products derived from crude petrol or oil. They disrupt the skin's natural immune barrier, impede elimination of toxins, promote acne/skin disorders, and cause the skin to prematurely age.

**Propylene glycol (PG)** (1,2- Propanedial), is the active ingredient in antifreeze. It is a petroleum derivative that weakens cellular structure. It is strong enough to remove barnacles from boats and is an eye, throat, respiratory tract, and skin irritant. Like aluminum, which is also commonly used in deodorants, PG stops the body's natural perspiration process. This traps toxins in the lymph and contributes to breast cancer.

**Sodium Lauryl Sulphate**, found in nearly all shampoos, can cause eye and scalp irritation, and swelling of the hands, face and arms. SLES is commonly contaminated with dioxin, a known carcinogen. The sodium lauryl sulfate found in our soaps is exactly the same as that found in a car wash or even a garage, where it is used to degrease car engines. It is believed to be responsible for many health problems ranging from PMS and menopausal symptoms to dropping male fertility and increasing female cancers.

# Fasting for Health

As our bodies are often bombarded by toxins in this modern world, fasting is an excellent way to remove them. In ayurveda, fasting is considered to be one of the most potent forms of healing. It can remove the seed of disease by dissolving accumulated toxins.

Accumulation is the first stage of sickness in disease pathology.

To people of good health, Amma recommends fasting once a week. This gives the body time to cleanse itself, enkindles digestive fire, and balances metabolism. As it reduces toxins in the body, mental clarity and physical strength increase. Fasting is also an excellent way to help the body fight off illness, especially colds, viruses, and infections. It is best to begin eating lighter foods, or even to fast completely, at the first sign of illness. Fasting gives the body immense power to rejuvenate itself. Best is fasting on water. If that is not possible, herbal teas, juices, or coconut water can be taken.

Amma also makes the point that the digestive system is like a machine that, unless we fast, never gets any rest. Any machine that runs 24 hours a day for years on end is prone to a break down sooner or later. Fasting once a week gives the digestive system its needed day of rest.

Longer fasts should be undertaken with guidance from experienced healthcare practitioners, as the foods taken before and after longer fasts have a powerful impact on the body.

*Ayurvedic Nutrition*

# Panchakarma Dietary Suggestions

Panchakarma is an ayurvedic method of deep cleansing at the cellular level. Panchakarma means "five actions." It removes toxins from both the physical body and the subtle body. It has a powerful detoxifying and rejuvenating effect on the bones, nerves, muscles, senses, and mind.

A proper diet is essential during panchakarma. The body is going through a deep transformation, and the right diet is essential in supporting this process. However, an improper diet prevents proper cleansing and can even drive existing toxins deeper.

The ideal diet to support panchakarma consists of light, nourishing, and easily digestible foods, such as vegetables and kichari. It is best to avoid eating after 6 pm, as the body's digestive fire is lower at this time. Food consumed at night goes undigested, forming ama (toxins). If it is absolutely necessary to eat at night, take rice water (kanji) or vegetable broth.

The following dietary recommendations are intended to support individuals doing panchakarma treatments under the guidance of experienced practitioners.

## *Foods That Assist the Purification Process*

- kichari (yellow mung dhal and basmati rice cooked with ghee and mild spices)
- steamed vegetables or lightly cooked non-spicy vegetables
- mild vegetable soup
- drink a minimum of 2-3 liters of water daily to help flush out toxins
- drink coconut water – young coconut meat (jelly) is okay in moderation
- ghee with food – 1 tsp (kapha), 1.5 tsp (pitta), 1 tbsp (vata) per meal maximum
- non-wheat porridge made with grains such as whole oats or ragi
- plain idly or dosa
- kanji (rice water)
- herbal teas: tulasi, ginger, cardamom, cinnamon, other tea according to dosha
- grape juice (without added sugar)

## Foods to Limit (OK in Moderation) During Panchakarma

- limit orange, pineapple, and pomegranate juice (without added sugar)
- buttermilk is okay once or twice a week
- limit nuts (almonds raw, soaked, and peeled – only 10 per day), no nuts for pitta
- limit salty and pungent (garlic, onion, chillies) foods
- limit sour foods (pickles, vinegar, and citrus)

## Foods to Completely Avoid During Panchakarma

- dairy (milk, curd, chai, butter, etc.) clogs the channels and inhibit detoxification
- fried food
- processed sugar
- tea, coffee, and stimulants
- very spicy food
- cold items such as ice cream, soda, water, and juice
- eggs, cheese, and soy products
- all wheat products and yeast products (such as uppama, bread, pasta, cookies, muffins)
- raw food

- vata-inducing vegetables (cauliflower, broccoli, cabbage, chickpeas)
- nightshade vegetables (potatoes, tomatoes, eggplant, bell peppers)
- mushrooms
- peanuts and peanut butter

Note: The above food recommendations are general guidelines and are not specific to dosha. It may be necessary to alter some of these to address your body's individual needs.

# Eating with Awareness

*"Never overeat. Half the stomach should be for food, a quarter for liquid, and the remaining portion for the movement of air. The less food you eat, the more mental control you will have. Do not sleep or meditate immediately after eating; if you do, you won't be able to digest the food properly. Always mentally repeat your mantra while you eat. This will purify the food and your mind at the same time."*

– Amma

The environment in which we eat, the thoughts we have while eating, and our habitual patterns during

## Ayurvedic Nutrition

meals affect our health as much as what we are eating. Ayurveda recommends eating in a clean, settled, and quiet atmosphere. Take a moment before eating to give thanks for the food, quiet your mind, and be in the present moment. Working, reading, watching TV, and excessive talking during meal times distract the body and mind from digestion. Eating when emotionally imbalanced or stressed hampers the digestive process, while eating food prepared with loving intention increases vitality. The digestive process begins in the mouth, so as Mahatma Gandhi said, "Chew your drinks and drink your food." By chewing food until it is ground into liquid in the mouth, less energy is required from the stomach.

How much we eat and the times when we eat also have a huge impact upon our well-being. Amma constantly emphasizes that we should not waste food. It is better to start with small portions than to throw out uneaten food. It is beneficial to avoid eating meals immediately after physical exertion or when there is no appetite. The organs function differently at various points in the day. The body can best assimilate breakfast from 6 – 8 am, lunch from 10 am – 2 pm, and dinner from 5 – 7 pm. It is also important to give each meal enough time to

*Eating with Awareness*

digest before taking in more food. Ayurveda suggests allowing approximately 3 to 6 hours between meals.

When we eat after 7 pm, the body has stopped producing most digestive enzymes; therefore, food eaten in the evening remains undigested in the stomach overnight, preventing the other organs from revitalizing themselves fully. This undigested food turns into toxic waste matter and makes us feel tired and dull in the morning. Skipping dinner is one of the best ways to regulate metabolism, balance weight, and help the body regenerate itself quickly. If you are extremely hungry at night, try a light soup, or herbal tea. Most people find that eating less at night provides more clarity and energy for the following day.

What we drink with our meals also plays a huge role in the digestive process. Consuming chilled/iced drinks at any time extinguishes the digestive fire. Drinking during meals dilutes digestive enzymes. It is best to drink nothing with meals. If you must have liquid with meals, then take herbal tea or warm/room-temperature water 10-15 minutes before or 30 minutes after eating. Drinking at the end of a meal greatly impedes digestion. Avoid meals when thirsty and avoid water while hungry.

## *Ayurvedic Nutrition*

Ayurveda recommends structuring each meal to include all six tastes: sweet, sour, salty, bitter, pungent, and astringent. Each taste has its own harmonizing effect; and including some of each minimizes cravings and balances the appetite and digestion. Most of the world tends to eat too much of the sweet, sour, and salty, and not enough of the bitter, pungent, and astringent tastes. Using multiple spices keeps meals simple while balancing the six tastes.

When considering what to eat, choose foods that are sattvic, whole, fresh, in-season, and locally grown whenever possible. Avoid eating too many heavy foods or too little light foods. Consumption of excessively hot food leads to weakness. Excessive cold and dry food leads to delayed digestion. Overcooking destroys nutrients and reduces vitality of food. Re-cooking food or allowing it to sit uncovered for long periods of time also devitalizes it.

In addition to beginning meals with awareness, it is advised to finish meals with mindfulness. Eat to about ¾ your capacity. Do not leave the table very hungry or very full. After eating, take a few minutes to sit quietly before returning to activity.

# Foods for Healing Illness

There is profound truth in the well-known expression "Let food be thy medicine." The following chart provides very basic suggestions for dietary remedies for various illnesses. This is not an all-inclusive chart. This is simply a list of foods that are helpful for people living with the listed conditions. Of course, taking these foods in combination with a medicinal/herbal program is even more beneficial!

| ILLNESS | HEALING FOODS |
|---|---|
| Allergies | Honey (local/raw), carrot, beet, spinach, celery, cayenne, grapes, nettles, garlic, onion, blueberries, ginger, horseradish. Avoid dairy, wheat, processed sugar, artificial chemicals and processed food. |
| Acne | Carrots, potato, burdock, spinach, grapes, seaweed, beets, cucumber |
| Anemia | Beets, carrots, dates, greens, berries, brown rice, pomegranate, burdock |
| Arthritis | Basmati rice, dhal with garlic, garlic chutney, milk with turmeric, kichari, steamed dark leafy vegetables, seaweeds, green superfoods |
| Asthma | Dhal, grapes, broccoli soup w/garlic, mustard, cumin, pepper, ginger milk |
| Bleeding Externally | Apply cayenne pepper to wound to stop bleeding |

## Ayurvedic Nutrition

| | |
|---|---|
| Bleeding Disorders | Saffron milk, coconut milk, rice pudding (calcium helps stop bleeding) |
| Boils | Turmeric (internally and externally), burdock, beets, greens, seaweeds |
| Cancer | Tulasi, Essiac Tea (see www.essiac.org), fresh vegetable juices, greens, fresh fruit juices, turmeric, oregano, berries, burdock, cilantro, parsley, daikon, nettles, avoid meat/fats/processed foods |
| Candida | Cooked garlic, dark greens, seaweeds, eliminate wheat/dairy/white sugar/yeast |
| Constipation | Lots of water, fiber, vegetables, fruits, beet juice, prunes, prune juice |
| Cough | Lentil soup, broccoli/vegetable soup with garlic, mustard, cumin, ginger, citrus, onion, tulasi, miso, cardamom, fennel |
| Diabetes | Millet, corn, leafy greens, bitter melon, berries, okra, turmeric, beans, bay leaf, tulasi, cinnamon, clove, cumin, coriander, no wheat/rice |
| Diarrhea | Rice, under-ripe bananas, grains |
| Dysentery | Same as diarrhea with a pinch of nutmeg |
| Earache | Garlic oil (boil garlic in sesame oil until it turns brown) 5 drops in the ears |
| Eyes | Warm black or chamomile tea bags soothe tired/swollen eyes, carrots, kale, pumpkin |
| Fever | Soft cooked unpolished rice, tapioca, tulasi leaves |

## Foods for Healing Illness

| Food Poisoning | Honey, live yogurt, coriander, turmeric, ginger |
|---|---|
| Flu/Cold | Tulasi, ginger, black pepper, cardamom, and cinnamon tea, garlic |
| Gall Bladder | Alfalfa, burdock, daikon, sprouts, aloe, dandelion greens, anise, walnuts |
| Headaches | Lots of water, juice, lemon, protein such as hempseed, dhal, beans |
| Heart Disease | Alfalfa, carrots, root vegetables, dark leafy greens, whole grains, red cabbage, beans, apples, berries, avoid meat/dairy |
| Hemorrhoids | Oatmeal, beans, turmeric, aloe vera, beets, pomegranate, no night shades |
| High Blood Pressure | Basmati rice, mung dhal, kichari, cilantro, coconut water, diuretic herb tea |
| High Blood Sugar | Lentils, dark leafy greens, beans, cayenne, cinnamon, turmeric, burdock, daikon, radishes, seaweeds, green superfoods, reduce fruit |
| High Cholesterol | Avocados, oats, alfalfa, whole grains, apples, hempseed/oil, figs, garlic |
| Hyperthyroid | Aloe vera, kelp, seaweeds, red lentil soup, dark leafy greens |
| Hypothyroid | Aloe vera, kelp, seaweeds, barley, miso, root vegetables, red cabbage |
| IBS | Kichari, lentils, okra, psyllium, avoid wheat/gluten/nuts/seeds/dairy, aloe vera |
| Immune Deficiency | Alfalfa, greens, garlic, fruits, berries, fruits, burdock, superfoods |

## Ayurvedic Nutrition

| | |
|---|---|
| Insomnia | Garlic milk with pinch of turmeric, nutmeg, whole grains |
| Joint Problems | Alfalfa, spinach, ginger, quinoa, turmeric, amaranth, parsley, rosemary, yams, root vegetables, blueberries, ghee, hempseed oil |
| Kidney Deficiency | Watermelon (unless edema), asparagus, parsley, lettuce, kidney beans, nettles, dark leafy greens, beets, celery, less salt |
| Liver Toxicity | Raw sugarcane juice(cleanses liver), cabbage, beets, daikon, radishes |
| Menopause | Leafy green vegetables, yam, basil, seaweeds, carrots, beans, oats |
| Migraines | Ripe banana cooked w/ghee/cardamom/nutmeg, nutmeg paste on forehead |
| Obesity | Grapefruit, salad, steamed veggies, beets, cabbage, green (unripe) and ripe papaya, ginger, pepper, berries, radishes |
| Osteoporosis | Greens, asparagus, quinoa, amaranth, apples, bananas, seaweeds, almonds, avoid pasteurized/homogenized dairy |
| Parasites/Worms | Pumpkin seeds, papaya seeds, garlic, brown rice, apricot seeds, avoid sugar/fruit/wheat/gluten/alcohol |
| Premenstrual Issues | Beans, seaweeds, carrots, apples, burdock, beets, raw cacao, avoid caffeine and alcohol |
| Rashes | Garlic, turmeric, cabbage, pears, red grapes, nettles, cucumbers, green papaya, tulasi, watermelon, ghee can be applied topically |

| Reproductive System | Garlic, onion, raw milk, almonds, dates, cashews, beets, burdock |
|---|---|
| Skin Problems (eczema, psoriasis) | Cilantro juice, cucumber juice internally and externally, rub inner side of cantaloupe on skin, pomegranate juice, avocado, papaya, aloe, berries, avoid dairy/wheat/processed sugar |
| Sore Throat | Lemon, ginger and honey tea, cayenne, also see flu/cold section |
| Stress | Tulasi tea, berries, miso, seaweeds, supergreen foods, dark leafy greens, yams, pumpkin, cooked apples, red grapes, raw warm turmeric milk |
| Stomach Ache | Ginger juice/soup, papaya, peppermint, papaya seeds, miso |
| Stomach Ulcers | Red cabbage juice, brown rice, steamed greens, kichari, berries, all alkaline food, avoid wheat/hot spices/caffeine/alcohol/processed sugar |
| Toothache | Clove, raw garlic (chew or hold in the mouth), parsley, wheatgrass juice |
| Urinary Tract Infection | Cranberry juice (without sugar), watercress, cucumber, berries, lemon, nettles, burdock, dandelion, brown rice, kichari |
| Vomiting/Nausea | Rice water, ginger, mint, honey |

# Conclusion

*And he knew that food was Brahman.
From food all beings are born,
By food they live and into food they return.*
Taittiriya Upanishad 3.2

We hear Amma constantly reminding us that we are not the body; we are the Atma (the Supreme Self). So why bother to eat healthily? These bodies are vehicles for transporting the soul. Just as we would not put gasoline mixed with dirt into our cars, we should consider what type of fuel we put into our soul's vehicle.

At the same time, we should be careful not to take our diets so seriously that we lose a sense of gratitude for whatever foods we receive. Our thoughts and attitude during meals affect our digestion and assimilation as much as the food itself. We are blessed if we have enough food to provide energy and nutrition. Millions of people do not have this.

We have infinite potential to heal ourselves and the planet by making some simple changes to our dietary habits. Amma again and again reflects to us that Mother Nature is very much out of balance.

*Conclusion*

She constantly encourages us to help restore that balance. By Her Grace, may we each find that balance internally and externally.

*Om brahmarpanam brahma havir brahmagnau
brahmana hutam brahmaiva tena gantavyam
brahma karma samadhina*

Brahman is the oblation,
Brahman is the food offering,
By Brahman it is offered into the fire of Brahman,
Brahman is that which is to be attained
By complete absorption (samadhi) in the action of Brahman.

Bhagavad Gita, 4:24

*Om Lokah Samastah Sukhino Bhavantu*

May All Beings Everywhere Be Happy

# Suggested Reading

*Ayurvedic Healing: A Comprehensive Guide (David Frawley)*
*Ayurveda: The Science of Healing (Vasant Lad)*
*Ayurvedic Cooking (Vasant Lad)*
*Diet for a New America (John Robbins)*
*Diet for a New World (John Robbins)*
*Healing with Whole Foods (Paul Pitchford)*
*Prakriti (Robert Svoboda)*
*Quantum Healing (Deepak Chopra)*
*Vegan Fusion (Mark Reinfeld)*
*Why Vegan? (visit www.VeganOutreach.com)*
*Yoga and Ayurveda (David Frawley)*

www.ingramcontent.com/pod-product-compliance
Lightning Source LLC
Chambersburg PA
CBHW061339040426
42444CB00011B/2997